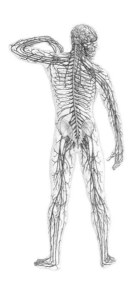

Feel, Think, Move

by Jana Martin

PEARSON

Scott
Foresman

Editorial Offices: Glenview, Illinois • Parsippany, New Jersey • New York, New York
Sales Offices: Needham, Massachusetts • Duluth, Georgia • Glenview, Illinois
Coppell, Texas • Ontario, California • Mesa, Arizona

ISBN: 0-328-13552-6

4 5 6 7 8 9 10 V0G1 14 13 12 11 10 09 08 07 06

A Remarkable System

Do you ever wonder what's going on inside your body when you hit a baseball or kick a soccer ball? Your brain is telling the rest of your body what to do. But without the muscles and bones in your body, you wouldn't be able to do either activity or even stand upright. Your muscles and bones make up an amazing system known as the **musculoskeletal** system. Working together, muscles and bones enable the human body to move.

The musculoskeletal system enables you to zip up your coat, open the door, and go outside to play. But how does your brain and the musculoskeletal system communicate? In fact, they are always communicating—even when you're asleep. Just about everything you do today, tomorrow, and every day is a result of communication between your brain and your muscles and bones.

The Brain

Let's start with your brain, which is housed inside your skull. Your skull is made of hard bone that protects the brain from injury. The brain is where your thoughts and emotions originate and where you make decisions. But there's a lot more going on than you might think.

The brain is a relatively small **organ** of the human body when you consider all that it does. On average, the human brain weighs three pounds. If a woman weighs 150 pounds, the brain makes up only two percent of her total body weight. The brain doesn't look very imposing either. It looks like a large, pinkish-gray, mushy walnut. But the brain is the leader of the rest of the body—the captain, so to speak. The rest of your body would be the obeying troops.

Everything in your body works together. Every organ and body part is a member of a system. The brain is no exception. It's part of the nervous system.

The nervous system includes the brain, the spinal cord, and the nerves. The spinal cord follows your spine, or backbone. The spinal cord is like a main communications cable or a two-way information highway. It sends messages from the brain to the rest of your body, and it sends signals from the rest of your body to your brain. Thirty-one pairs of spinal nerves extend from the sides of the spinal cord and branch out into smaller and smaller bunches of nerves, reaching every part of your body.

How do the different parts of your body communicate? Through **neurons**! Neurons are nerve cells that transmit signals around your body at up to 200 miles an hour. There are neurons in your brain, speeding around. When a neuron "fires," it sparks a reaction in your brain, which then sends signals to other neurons. This sends a message to certain muscles in your body to contract. When your muscles contract, your body moves.

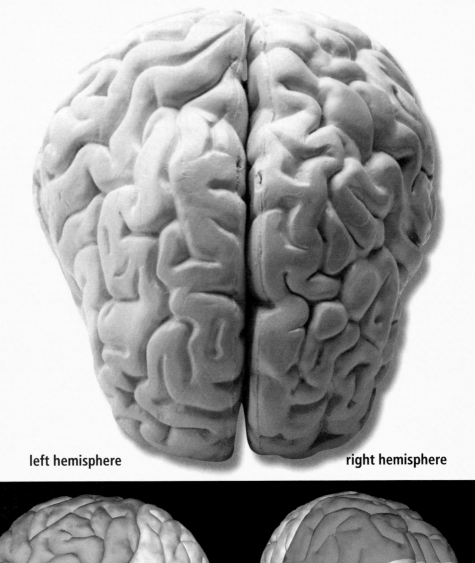

left hemisphere   right hemisphere

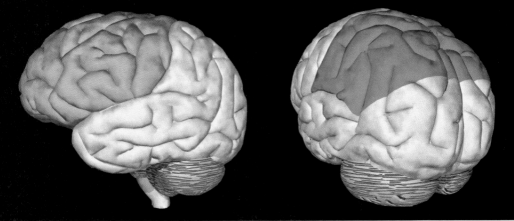

frontal lobe (movement, speech,   parietal lobe (pain)
emotions); part of this is the motor
cortex (controls movement)

Let's take a closer look at your brain. It's divided down the center into two halves, called the **cerebral hemispheres**.

Each half is divided into four parts, called lobes:

- **frontal lobe:** enables you to plan, speak, feel emotions, solve problems, and move. Within the frontal lobe is the motor cortex, which is responsible for sending messages down your spinal cord and to your muscles. This allows you to move different parts of your body.
- **parietal lobe:** enables you to perceive pain and different temperatures.
- **occipital lobe:** helps you to see through your eyes.
- **temporal lobe:** where your memory is stored. It also enables you to understand what you hear.

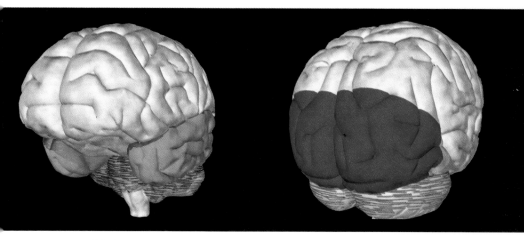

occipital lobe (sight)

temporal lobe
(memory, comprehension)

Swing, Batter, Swing!

1. John's eyes see the ball approaching and convert the image into electrical impulses that are sent to his brain.

2. Occipital lobe in the brain gets a signal from his eyes.

3. The temporal lobe remembers what he had done in the past and what his coach has told him about the right way to swing.

4. The frontal lobe processes information about time and distance, and then the motor cortex sends a signal down the spinal cord to different muscles in the legs and arms.

5. His muscles receive the signal and swing!

The Musculoskeletal System

Now let's take a closer look at the musculoskeletal system. It's actually made up of two different systems: the muscular system and the skeletal system, or your muscles and your bones. These systems work together to help you sit, stand, walk, run, and play your favorite sport.

The Skeletal System

The skeletal system is the frame of the human body. Can you visualize the scary skeleton you see at Halloween? Each of us has a skeleton like that inside. You just can't see it because it is covered with muscles, blood, and skin.

There are 206 bones of different shapes and sizes in your body. Inside those bones is a softer center that contains bone marrow, which produces red blood cells and white blood cells. The skeletal system also includes the connective tissues that fasten those bones together. There are three main types of connective tissue: cartilage, tendons, and ligaments. Bones are made of collagen, a type of protein, and calcium. Calcium is what keeps bones hard. Connective tissue has collagen, but no calcium.

It's hard to imagine how eating a food could have a direct effect on your body, but foods that have calcium are very important for your bones. If you eat more calcium, you are increasing the amount of calcium in your bones. That will make your bones stronger.

But how much calcium should you have? People between the ages of 9 and 18 should eat 1300 milligrams of calcium every day. And where do you get it? In fact, many foods have calcium. But some foods have more than others.

Recommended Calcium Intakes

Food	Serving Size	Calcium
Yogurt	1 cup	450 mg
Fat-free milk	1 cup	352 mg
Calcium-fortified orange juice	1 cup	333 mg
Macaroni and cheese	1/2 cup	181 mg
Tofu	1/2 cup	130 mg
Soy beverage	1 cup	300 mg
Broccoli	1 cup	90 mg
Spinach, boiled	1 cup	244 mg
Almonds	1 ounce (20–25 Almonds)	71 mg

Connectors

Connective tissue is softer than bone and keeps the major bones in a person's body together. One type of connective tissue is cartilage.

Another type of connective tissue is the tendon. Tendons, like tough cords connecting muscles to bones, allow the muscles to pull on bones, causing movement. Try wiggling your fingers as you look at the top of your hand. Those lines you see on the back of your hand are tendons. They attach your fingers to your wrist and move when you move your fingers.

The third type of connective tissue is the ligament, which connects bones with other bones. Ligaments are found in joints. A joint is where two major bones come together, and it is usually a point of movement. Knees, ankles, and elbows are examples of joints.

These girls scramble to get to the soccer ball first. Their knees are the most important joints in their bodies for this sport.

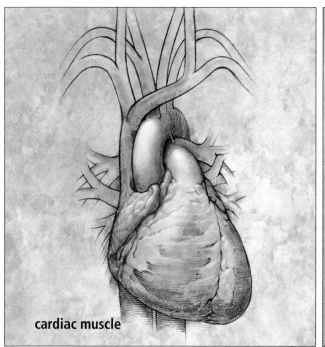

cardiac muscle

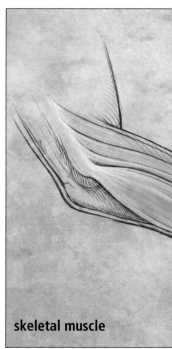

skeletal muscle

Muscles

Do you ever wonder why sometimes your body moves without you thinking about it moving? For example, have you ever had the shivers or an eye twitch? Or have you ever been to the doctor and felt your leg jump after the doctor taps your knee with a hammer?

The reason this happens is that you have different types of muscles in your body. Some of them you control voluntarily. Others move involuntarily.

You have three types of muscles:
- cardiac muscles
- skeletal muscles (also called voluntary muscles)
- smooth muscles

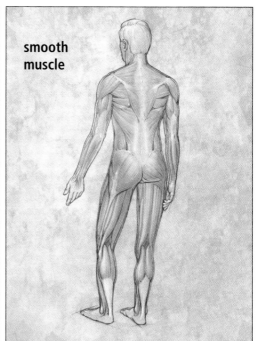

smooth
muscle

Skeletal muscles move bones and hold your skeletal system upright. These muscles are generally attached to two or more bones, either directly or with tendons. Where they are attached to bones at a joint, they work in opposing pairs. This means one muscle contracts to bend a joint, and the other contracts to straighten it. These are the muscles you are usually aware that you are using.

Smooth muscles, on the other hand, are muscles that are often working without your knowledge. They move substances around, such as blood through your blood vessels and food through your digestive system.

The final type of muscles, cardiac muscles, make up the wall of your heart. They help pump blood and regulate your heartbeat rate. They are working all the time, without any action on your part.

There are more than 600 muscles in the human body. They make up, on average, half of a person's body weight. Each muscle has its own name.

- Muscles that bend are called flexors.
- Muscles that straighten are called extensors.
- Muscles that move a limb to the side, away from the body, are abductors.
- Muscles that move a limb closer to the body are called adductors.

It's probably a surprise to you, but your face has numerous muscles. They are working nearly all the time. You use them every time you smile and every time you frown. Unlike other muscles, facial muscles do not attach directly to bone. Instead, they attach under skin.

There's another muscle group that you probably don't think about very often. You can't tone it by going to the gym. In fact you can't really exercise it at all. That muscle is your tongue! The tongue is actually made up of a group of muscles that work together to allow you to talk and chew food.

Motor Skills

What are motor skills? They have to do with a person's ability to control his or her muscles. Motor skills improve naturally as we grow. They can also be improved by practice.

When a baby is born, he has little control over his muscles. But, as he grows, he gains more and more ability to move—called motor skills. As his motor skills develop, he learns to crawl, then stand, then walk, and then run.

How We Grow

Before puberty, boys and girls have a very similar shape. But during their teenage years, they go through what is called a growth spurt. They both change shape noticeably. Usually, for boys, this can mean growing taller by as much as 3.5 inches (9 cm) a year. Usually, for girls, this can mean growing at a rate of 3.15 inches (8 cm) a year.

We don't grow all at once. The hands and feet grow first. Then the arms and legs grow. The spine, or backbone, is the last part to grow. As a result of these rapid changes, many teenagers need to buy new shoes and clothes often. This also explains why some teenagers may feel less coordinated. Their bodies are growing so fast, and their brains have a hard time adjusting.

Girls usually finish this growth spurt before boys do. By the age of fourteen, most girls have reached their adult height. Boys, on the other hand, won't finish growing until around age twenty. Because they have more years to grow, adult men are, on average, 5.12 inches (13 cm) taller than women.

Another reason for their height is that boys grow faster than girls at their peak rate, which is in their mid-teenage years. The final phase of skeletal growth in boys is a broadening of the chest and shoulders. In general, a man's bones are also denser and heavier than a woman's.

A Lean, Mean Machine

What makes an athlete great? At 6 feet 5 inches tall, professional basketball player Lisa Leslie towers over many of her teammates and competitors, but her physical stature isn't the only reason for her success. Experts agree that her success is a result of many things: her strength, her height, her attitude, and her determination.

Lisa Leslie has superb **coordination** between her brain and her musculoskeletal system. How do you know? One sign is her ability to slam-dunk. In fact, she's the first woman to slam-dunk in a professional game. She says she gets her strength and skill from her mother, who is 6 feet 3 inches tall. But she also practices—all the time. That keeps her muscles moving, her brain working, and her bones strong.

This basketball superstar went to high school in Los Angeles, where she was a star player. A member of the WNBA team, the Los Angles Sparks, she's also been on the USA Olympic team. She has been on nine USA gold-medal winning teams and has averaged sixteen points per game.

What Is Physical Therapy, and Why Does It Work?

As people age, their bones and muscles naturally become weaker. It is common for elderly people to have surgery to replace certain joints. Hips, knees, and backs often cause older people pain. This can happen when you're younger, too. Physical therapy can help people relearn how to walk or use different parts of their bodies after surgery.

In addition to working with patients, physical **therapists** sometimes recommend exercise classes, swimming, and massage therapy.

Sometimes your favorite athlete gets injured, and you don't see him or her on the court or field for a while. Maybe he pulled a tendon, or maybe she sprained an ankle. As part of the healing process, professional athletes often see a physical therapist. A physical therapist helps people recover from

accidents that affect their ability to move or use certain body parts.

Physical therapists help old and young patients alike.

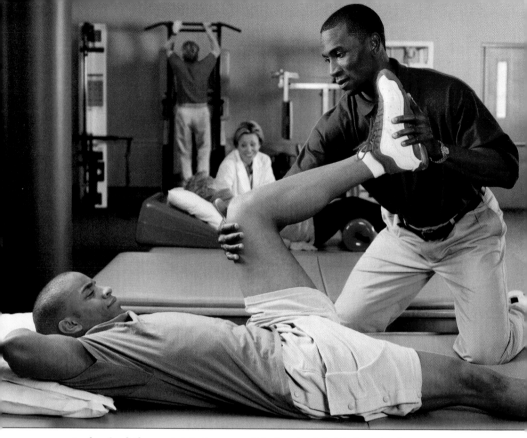

A physical therapist helps an athlete stretch his leg during treatment for an injury.

Physical therapists use a wide range of treatments, and they treat all types of people—old, young, fit, inactive. Sometimes they have patients exercise to increase flexibility or strength. Other times they use heat or cold to reduce pain. And sometimes they massage muscles to increase blood circulation.

One thing physical therapists are good at is helping people relearn how to use a limb or joint after an accident or surgery. A person's brain may remember how to walk, but a weakness in a leg may prevent it. A physical therapist works with the person until the brain and musculoskeletal system are working together again.

Summary

In this book, you have learned how the brain communicates with the musculoskeletal system to enable you to move. You also looked at what makes up the brain and the musculoskeletal systems. You learned about the bones and muscles in the human body. There are 206 bones and more than 600 muscles in total. You learned how people grow, how people move, what happens when they need to learn how to move again, and even what makes them great. You also learned something about nutrition. If you exercise and eat healthily, you can improve the strength of your bones and muscles.

Together, your brain and musculoskeletal system allow you to move. They enable you to do everything from standing up, to riding a bike, to playing a musical instrument or flying a kite. What else do they enable you to do?

Now Try This

Taking a Closer Look

Pick one part of the body. It could be a shoulder, arm, knee, leg, wrist, foot, or hand. You could even pick the **abdomen** or the back.

Now you're going to play musculoskeletal detective. Your job is to identify the major muscles and bones that make up that part of the body. In other words, you're going to take the part of the human body you picked and find out the major bones and muscles that it includes.

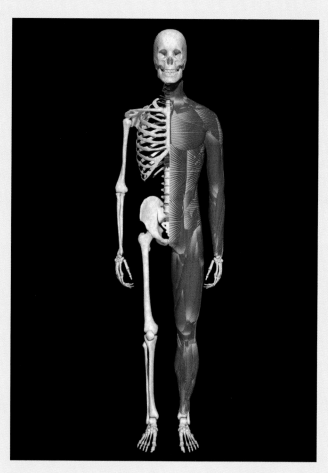

1. To do so, you will need to do some research. Go on the Internet or go to the library. You need to look for anatomical diagrams. These are scientific drawings of the human body that feature the musculoskeletal system. Make sure these drawings have labels of muscles and bones. If you are going to focus on the back of the body, make sure you find a diagram of the back of the body. If you are going to focus on the front of the body, make sure you find a diagram that shows that.

2. Then, write a list of the bones and muscles in that part of the body. What muscles are connected to what bones? For instance, what muscle wraps around the shoulder blade? What muscles are connected to the thighbone? Your list should give a full picture of the way that part of the body's muscles and bones work together.

   You've solved the mystery of what makes up that part of your body!

Glossary

abdomen *n.* the section of the body that holds the intestines and stomach; the belly.

cerebral hemispheres *n.* left and right symmetrical halves of the brain, each of which controls the opposite side of the body.

coordination *n.* the working together of muscles for easy movement.

musculoskeletal *adj.* made up of a combination of the muscles and the skeleton.

neurons *n.* main cells of the nervous system.

organ *n.* an internal part of the body that performs a specific function.

therapists *n.* specialists who provide treatment of an illness or disability through exercise and massage.